Written by Kit Frost.
Illustrations by Steve James, Chris Dickason
and Emiliano Migliardo.
Cover artwork based on designs by Thy Bui.

First published in Great Britain in 2026 by Red Shed, part of Farshore

An imprint of HarperCollins*Publishers*
1 London Bridge Street, London SE1 9GF
www.farshore.co.uk

HarperCollins*Publishers*
Macken House, 39/40 Mayor Street Upper, Dublin 1, D01 C9W8, Ireland

Red Shed is a registered trademark of HarperCollins*Publishers* Ltd.

Copyright © HarperCollins*Publishers* Limited 2026

ISBN 978 0 00 882549 2

Printed and bound in Great Britain by Clays Ltd, Elcograf S.p.A.

1

A CIP catalogue record for this title is available from the British Library.

MIX
Paper | Supporting
responsible forestry
FSC
www.fsc.org
FSC® C018072

AMAZING JOKES

FOR

EVERY 8 YEAR OLD

RED SHED

Whether you love animals, science or sport, you'll find LOADS of hilarious jokes in this book to make you laugh your head off . . .

Why did the leopard wear dark clothes?

What's a bun's favourite type of music?

What did one sheep say to the other?

Read on to find out the answers – and get ready to giggle.

Why don't you ever see
elephants hiding in trees?

Because they are so good at hiding.

Why did the boy throw the clock out of his window?

He wanted to see time fly.

What do you call a chicken who tells jokes?

A comedi-hen.

What did the tomato do when he was behind in the running race?

He tried to ketchup.

Why are pine trees awful at sewing?

Because they always drop their needles.

Why is a broken drum a great gift?

Because you just can't beat it.

What illness do Christmas trees get?

Tinsel-itis.

How do you decide how long to mow your lawn for?

Use an hour-grass.

What's the lawn's favourite party game?

Hide and seed.

Why do bees have sticky hair?

Because they use a honeycomb.

What did the ocean say when she saw her friend?

Nothing, she just waved.

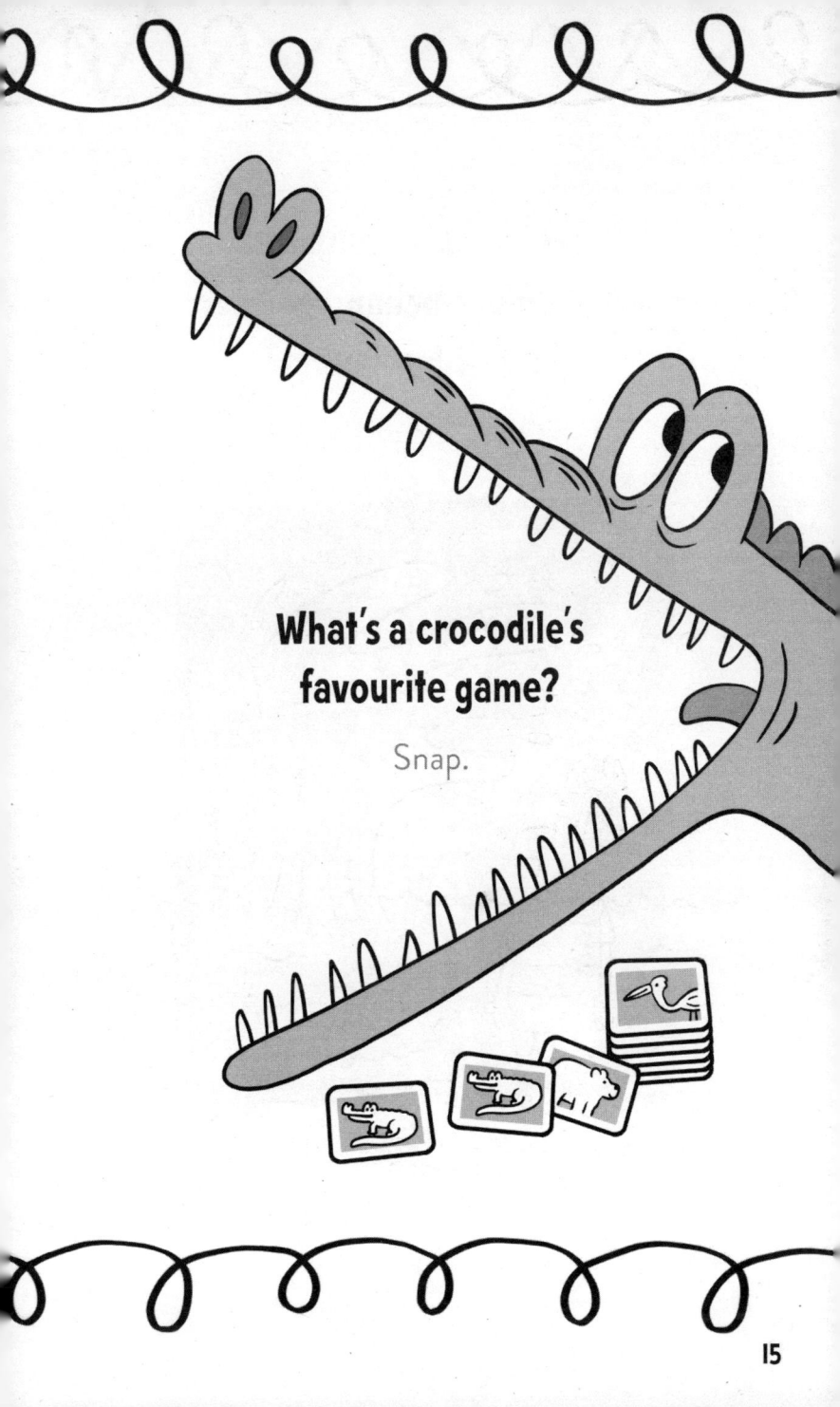

What's a crocodile's favourite game?

Snap.

What books do vampires like reading?

Ones they can really sink their teeth into.

Why did the bird go to the library?

To try and find some book worms.

Why wasn't the librarian allowed on the plane?

It was overbooked.

What's a bun's favourite type of music?

Rock and roll.

Which part of a snake weighs the most?

Its scales.

Why do dogs make great comedians?

They always paws in the right places.

Why did the cat start playing piano?

It loved the mew-sic.

What did the snowman say to his friend?

Can you smell carrots?

How do snowmen get around?

By icicle.

What did the teacher say to the naughty bee in the class?

Bee-hive yourself.

**What do you call
a hard-working dinosaur?**

A Try-ceratops.

Why was the maths book unhappy?

It had a lot of problems.

Maths

26

What's an astronaut's favourite part of a laptop?

The space key.

What was wrong with the restaurant on the Moon?

There was no atmosphere.

What's a ship's captain's least
favourite vegetable?

A leek.

How did the tree get onto the internet?

It logged in.

What did the egg say when it heard a joke?

I'm cracking up.

**Where did the man with the
sweet tooth go on holiday?**

A dessert island.

Knock, knock.

Who's there?

Hatch.

Hatch who?

Bless you!

**What did the spider
say to the fly?**

Catch you later!

Where do owls stay on holiday?

In a hoot-el.

Two sausages were sizzling in a pan.
One said to the other, 'It's hot in here.'
The other one replied, 'Argh, it's
a talking sausage!'

Why did the pony get a telling-off?

Because it couldn't stop horsing around.

Why didn't the carpet trust the stairs?

It was always up to something.

Knock, knock.

Who's there?

Ben.

Ben who?

Ben knocking for half an hour!

Did you ever hear the joke about the bins?

It's rubbish!

What cat lives underwater?

An octo-puss.

What do storm clouds wear under their clothes?

Thunderwear.

What did one sheep say to the other sheep?

Nice to see ewe.

What did the rabbit say on her best friend's birthday?

Hoppy birthday!

What did the oyster say on its birthday?

It's time to shell-ebrate!

**Why did the snake
cross the road?**

To get to the other
ssssside.

Why didn't the skeleton go to the party?

It had no body to go with.

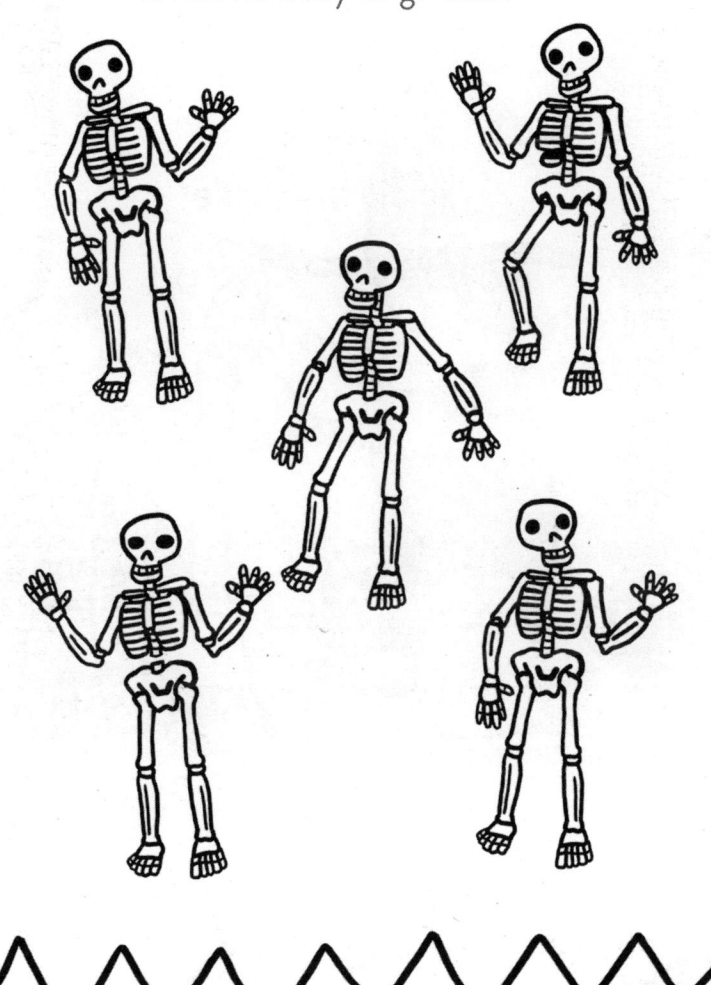

What do you call a witch on the beach?

A sand-witch.

Why is it good to tell jokes in lifts?

Because they work on many levels.

Knock, knock.

Who's there?

Lettuce.

Lettuce who?

Lettuce in, it's freezing!

What do you call a bear with no ears?

A 'B'.

Why do oranges wear sun cream?

So that their skin doesn't peel.

What did the pencil say to its friend?

You're looking sharp.

Who's king of the pencil case?

The ruler.

Knock, knock.

Who's there?

Needle.

Needle who?

Needle little help opening the door?

What's a horse's favourite sport?

Stable tennis.

What did the horse say to the horse next door?

You're my neigh-bour.

Cheep!
Cheep!

What's a bird's favourite type of restaurant?

Somewhere cheep.

Knock, knock.

Who's there?

Europe.

Europe who?

No, YOU'RE a poo!

What's a vampire's favourite fruit?

Blood oranges.

What's orange and sounds like a carrot?

A parrot.

Did you hear about the pirate who got a cheap flag?

It was in the sails.

What did the left eye say to the right eye?

Between you and me, something smells.

Knock, knock.

Who's there?

Cauliflower.

Cauliflower who?

Cauliflowers don't have
a last name, silly!

What type of tree is easiest to fit in your hand?

A palm tree.

What tool can you use to cut the sea?

A see-saw.

**What plates do aliens use
to eat their lunch?**

Flying saucers.

What do you call a fly that's stuck in your butter?

A butterfly.

What do you call a bear with no teeth?

A gummy bear.

Why was the ghost so bad at lying?

Everyone saw through him.

What do you call a bull having a nap?

A bull dozer.

Why did the star audition for the movie?

Because she wanted to be a movie star!

What's an astronaut's favourite fish?

A starfish.

What's a frog's favourite fast food order?

French flies.

Why did the piece of art go to prison?

It had been framed.

What's blue and not very heavy?

Light blue.

How many oranges grow on trees?

All oranges grow on trees!

What's a tornado's favourite game?

Twister.

Why did the man take a long time to eat a clock?

It was very time consuming.

What problem did the twin witches have?

No one could tell which witch was which.

What was the witch's best subject at school?

Spelling.

What's a vampire's favourite dessert?

Ice scream.

Why did the dinosaur cross the road?

Because chickens hadn't evolved yet.

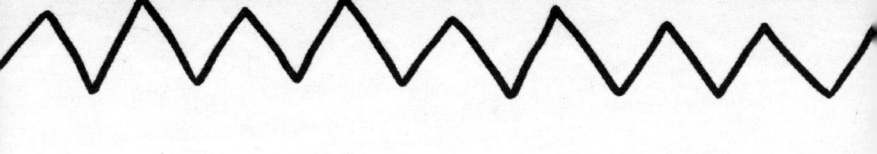

Why did the chicken cross the road?

Because the chicken it was standing
with had farted.

Why did the cockerel cross the road?

He had a lot to cock-a-doodle-doo!

What did the poo say to the fart?

You blow me away.

Why did the party guest bring toilet paper?

They were a real party pooper.

When is an apple not an apple?

When it's a pineapple.

Knock, knock.

Who's there?

Bean.

Bean who?

Bean a while since I saw you.

Which animal is best at playing cricket?

A bat.

Why are tennis players so noisy?

They're always making a racquet.

'Waiter, waiter, what's this fly doing in my soup?'

'It looks like it's learning to swim.'

A girl went to visit her friend and they decided to paint their nails. Before they started, the friend put on a jacket . . . and then another jacket.

'What are you doing?' the girl asked.

'The bottle said it works best if you put on two coats,' said the friend.

Why did the leopard wear dark clothing?

So she wouldn't be spotted.

Knock, knock.

Who's there?

Woo.

Woo who?

Woo hoooo, let's party!

What do you call a bear who's got caught in the rain?

A drizzly bear.

When can four elephants all stand under one umbrella and not get wet?

When it's not raining.

What's an elephant's favourite part of a tree?

The trunk.

How do elephants call each other?

On the ele-phone.

Why shouldn't you wear a cardboard belt?

Because it's a waist of paper.

What happened when the sheet of paper got stressed?

It folded under pressure.

Two friends, Sue and Mo, went to the aquarium together. Sue went straight in, while Mo looked around the gift shop. Sue came back out after a minute or two, saying it was time to go.

'Why?' said Mo.

'There's something fishy going on in there,' Sue replied.

Look out for other books in the series!

What sort of plant is the best at surprises?

An am-bush.